God, I Love You!

Prayers, Praise, and Promises from the Soul

HEIDI

Thank you so
much for your
love waiting with you
encouragement
with you

God, I Love You!

Prayers, Praise, and Promises from the Soul

Vykki Morrison

Dedicated
to my grandmother, Medora Fox,
to my darling,
and to Tom Tutton,
who gave me the idea

Acknowledgements

I would like to thank the following people
for making this book possible:

My wonderful Production Consultant, Ruth Marcus—
thanks for your kindness and holding my hand.

Beta Readers,
Glenn Barbieri, Rev. Kristin Luana Baumann,
and Robert Thompson—
I sincerely appreciate your suggestions.

My fellow writers, Heidi Hanson and Gordon Anderson—
thanks for the advice!

And finally, my sister and brother, who helped keep my head
from falling off every time it started spinning.

Table of Contents

"Let the words of my mouth,
and the meditation of my heart,
be acceptable in thy sight,
O Lord, my strength and my redeemer."
—*Psalms 19:14*

Introduction

It was through my grandmother I learned to say prayers.

My grandmother was a minister and a woman of fierce faith. Some of my earliest memories are of sleeping on hard, uncomfortable pews and waking to the sound of her voice quoting scripture or giving forth in resounding prayer. A small woman with a strong voice, I've always been certain that when she prayed, God stopped and listened.

During her sermons, she would quote the prayers of Biblical kings and prophets. She told of heartfelt, honest conversations of men in close relationships with their God, men so often painfully overwhelmed by circumstances of the day, asking for help. She also spoke of joyful songs of praise and bold words of faithful promise.

I loved those words, the flow and beauty in the King James version of the Bible—the power within the prayers themselves.

Those prayers taught me to trust and have faith; brought me solace through trying times. More than that, they gave me a foundation to base my life upon; to live a life of love, and the assurance that God, in whatever form it took, would always provide for me.

It wasn't only those written prayers that changed my life; my grandmother's prayers are with me still. Listening to her pray used to cause chills to run down me. Both the earnest way she spoke and the words she used helped me understand she was having a conversation with someone she believed in wholeheartedly, and moreover, that she loved.

Nana was not afraid to ask anything, nor was she stingy with her praise. A lifetime of difficulty had proven that she and God could get through anything. As well as worship, there was complete trust.

Many people today feel alienated from God, not knowing how to pray. They don't know how the old prayers relate to today's issues, or how they apply to their lives. They don't feel that those prayers represent what they're going through.

It's true that life today is different than it was thousands of years ago. The issues we face have changed through the ages, and today we're overwhelmed by situations such as drug abuse and mental illness. But prayer is still as important now as it was back then. Prayer gives us hope and helps us overcome.

Prayer is the foundation of our relationship with God, one that's individual and unique for each of us. It's an amazing journey, but one made more difficult when we don't know what to say or how to say it.

That's the reason I wrote this book. I want to share prayers about things that are important to us today. I want people to know that we can make humble prayers or bold requests, shout with joy, show God our anger or confusion. I want us to make promises of faithfulness to God and remember Gods' promises of faithfulness to us. And I want each of us to have the type of relationship with God that worshippers had thousands of years ago, that my grandmother had through her life. Heartfelt and real.

In this book I've included prayers of praise and thanksgiving, laments about troubles, promises to God and reminders of promises made by God. I've included some short pieces meant to be sung, and supplications: humble, and earnest requests. There are even prayers of confusion, of anger, and of fear.

As you read this book, if any of the prayers resonate with you, I encourage you to use them freely. On the opposite side of each prayer page is a space for that purpose: to make notes, write your own prayer, or to make each of these prayers your own.

Thank you.

Vykki

"Pray without ceasing."
—1 Thessalonians, 5:17

Use this page for notes or make this prayer your own.

Through the centuries Your name has been Our Prayer;
David sang songs in Your praise
Wrote poems, made supplications.
May my words touch Your heart today, God
In the way of David.

Use this page for notes or make this prayer your own.

I have listened to Your words,
I have searched the truth of them
With prayer and supplication.
I have washed my face and fasted,
I have entered into my closet and called upon
Your name
According to Your word,
That I may attain wisdom and knowledge.
You are my first thought
You are my last thought.
I see You in my dreams and in my awakenings.
How blessed I am to be always in
Your presence!
I praise You in all I see.

Use this page for notes or make this prayer your own.

God
Creator of my heart,
Before the earth was born
You spoke my name.
Today, in this moment
I hear Your voice.
I hear You and come running.

Use this page for notes or make this prayer your own.

Bless me, that my days are good
That laughter bubbles from my lips
That joy in You shines through my eyes.

For my feet are mired in fear, my God
I am knee deep in tribulation
I will drown in this river
If You don't take my hands,
Rescue my spirit, resuscitate my faith.

Wolves look over the ledge slavering for my blood
Vultures circle overhead scenting me dying
I am weak in my faith.
I will drown in this river
If You don't take my hands.

Use this page for notes or make this prayer your own.

This prayer is not for me
I spend this time upon my knees
In supplication, with tears
In love and with a loving heart
I hold him up in prayer.

This prayer is not for me
But a prayer warrior I will be
I ask of You, I trust in You
I know Your guidance is here
I hold him up in prayer.

This prayer is not for me
And I will pray till he is free
From the chains that hold him tight
I trust You and Your might
I hold him up in prayer.

Use this page for notes or make this prayer your own.

You are the God of my birth
The Strength of my rising years
You are the Word in my mouth
The desire of my heart.
I am a speck before You
But You are my love.

Use this page for notes or make this prayer your own.

Open my eyes,
Open my eyes, God,
Open my heart,
And my understanding.
Let Your light shine from every pore,
Let my eyes blaze Your love,
Open my chest and bring Yourself forth,
God, the I Am.

Use this page for notes or make this prayer your own.

Master.
God,
Owner of my being,
When I saw Your majesty
I fell before You.
A free woman, I enslaved my soul to You
My heart I manacled
With unbreakable chains.
Forever will I walk with You.

Use this page for notes or make this prayer your own.

God, I called Your name, but You did not answer.
Behind doors I looked for You
In dark, empty rooms.
I texted, tweeted, Facebooked You
But there is no God on social media.
Where then are You, where is Your voice?
I asked.
God said,
"I answered before you called"
And
"I am the room"
And
"You are my voice on social media."

Use this page for notes or make this prayer your own.

Cancer has me, God
I am weak and in pain.
I smile at those about me who look with pity;
My Cancer has them in pain as well.
I have fought long and fought ferociously,
I have given my very best in this war
But it is time to lay down arms.
Dearest God, forgive me for my fear,
For my anger and secret tears.
Remove from me this hate toward Cancer,
I know it hurries me to You.
But please send me angels to explain
Why me?
Please have them take my hands
As I make my visits to the hospital.
Have them speak to me of the calmness
That comes with acceptance.
Let them sing with me, praising You,
Though my voice is gone.
Take this cup from me if it is Your will,
And if it is not, bring me Your words of peace.

Use this page for notes or make this prayer your own.

There were clear skies with long vision yesterday
Today fog blinds me and there is rain without cease.
Direct my path, God
I cannot see before me.

Use this page for notes or make this prayer your own.

A child, one child amongst a thousand children
But this one is ours,
A true gift
Healthy and loud, perfect in complexion and soft of spirit
Ours to mold, to teach, to raise.
We will cherish and protect her;
She will teach us to be good parents.
Such awe and joy,
What have we done to be blessed with this gift of an Angel?

Use this page for notes or make this prayer your own.

Your song is on my lips
Your praise is on my tongue
My words are honey
Dripping with the sweetness of You
My prayers are the sunlight of Your praise.

Use this page for notes or make this prayer your own.

My soul is sore from the journey,
I have walked without stopping and I am limping.
My shoulders ache from my burden
I am bowed low.
Heal my soul with Your word.
God, my protector
My pain has been great.
I have hung by my fingernails
I have wept rivers of tears
Till my breath would not come
And my eyes were dry.
In desperation I cry to You,
God, rock of my salvation
Heal my soul.

Use this page for notes or make this prayer your own.

Touch me, and bring light to my life;
I will shine brightly as a lantern
I will illuminate all I shine upon
I will speak Your name in praise
Touch me, God.

Use this page for notes or make this prayer your own.

Where is Your mercy, God?
We are small and fragile Creatures
Before Your immenseness.
I take no solace in hearing
That You wanted him with You,
That it was his time.
My beautiful baby with eyes barely open
Who hardly met his parents
Why did You take what You had given me?
I am so angry, I am so angry at You.
You have taken my heart
My soul has withered, my tears have run out.
I am so angry, so angry at You.
Give him back!
Return my heart to me. Let my soul sing again.
I am so angry with You,
Yet even so, I am Yours always.

Use this page for notes or make this prayer your own.

Thy name be praised,
In ringing of bells, in chanting of voice
In singing of song.
We praise You in all Your names
We will worship You forever.

Use this page for notes or make this prayer your own.

I was brought up Godly
A preacher's kid to my very heart,
So, of course, I moved away
Stopped being good and started playing the world
But they never stopped praying for me.

I'm sure it was said
I was being prodigal
I played long, I played hard
Got too very angry to let them see
That I still needed someone praying for me.

I spit in their faces and I spit at the Word
I lived a full life without questions of God
Grew a family of my own, made money and mistakes
Bought a house but had no home.
But no matter the disappointments and the cares
They always held me in their prayers.

Then one day when I imploded
Feeling empty and alone
I remembered very faintly that I was brought up Godly.
I was embarrassed to be asking God,
Yet every day they bowed and prayed.
God said they held me in their prayers.

Use this page for notes or make this prayer your own.

The winds blow, the leaves rustle
And I hear Your voice.
The waves lap the shore
And I hear Your voice.
Speak clearly so I can understand.

Use this page for notes or make this prayer your own.

My Nana rocked me
On her lap
In the old rocking chair,
Back and forth she
Rocked into me
Your word, Your love,
Her love,
And her prayers.

My Nana rocked me
With my head against her breast
My arms around her neck,
My eyes tightly closed
And my heart content.
In the old rocking chair,
She rocked into me Your word
She rocked into me Your praise.

My Nana can no longer rock,
I have no chair to rock her.
Please pull her tight, dear God
Let her rest upon You,
And rock her in Your love.

Use this page for notes or make this prayer your own.

I heard someone say I was an angel.
Am I an angel, God?
You forgot to give me wings.
Angels are supposed to have wings.
And help people,
And fly above all the mean things that people say
And show love when kids make you bleed.
Are you sure I'm an angel, God?

Someone said I was a burden.
I figured out the word
A burden is someone who is slow and feels stupid
A burden makes her parents cry and get angry
I think a burden must be a mistake.
But You don't make mistakes, God,
I'm not slow about that
So maybe I am an angel, but not a full angel yet
Maybe I have to love and smile more to get wings.
I can do that.
I can smile when I am bullied;
I can pick myself up when people hurt me.
And You can give me wings to fly above the pain.

Use this page for notes or make this prayer your own.

Let my words be Glory
Glory, Glory to the Only
To the One, to the All
Glory, Glory to the Mighty
To Perfection, to the All
May my words be Glory.

Use this page for notes or make this prayer your own.

Do not shut me out, I pray; do not turn Your back
On my arrogance.
I have been without understanding, without caring,
And without righteousness.
I pray, please do not shut me out.
I can be fixed, I can do better, if You will but
Keep company with me.
I have hurt the hearts of those I love.
I have sown discord with my arrogance,
Have cut those I know
To the quick with one hundred shallow cuts.
I have caused tears to flow from innocence.
I see myself, and I am ashamed. Is there no hope for me?
I will lie under Your feet, God, and beg till I die
I will debase myself to You and punish myself forever
If You will not help me.

Use this page for notes or make this prayer your own.

God, I see You.
I bow to Your love.
You are my Everything.

Use this page for notes or make this prayer your own.

Children in my hands
Children raucous and misbehaving,
Thinking they know everything,
And I know nothing.
God, I pray for inspiration,
Pray for patience and love.
Please help me to be loving
When they know not love,
Patient when they are not,
Inspiring in my words and actions
As I try to hold their attention.
May I teach them more than subjects,
May my words give them thought,
May Your spirit touch their lives.
Amen.

Use this page for notes or make this prayer your own.

What wrong step did I take that put me here?
What is this test that brings me to my knees
And brings me shame?
What has me eating from dumpsters
Washing my clothes in gas station restrooms,
Which do not get clean and
Gives me a stench that keeps me in corners?
Are You going to rescue me, or is this my life now?
What did I do that put me here?
Is this Your choice for me? If so,
I will try to find Your love in this spot
While I beg for money to buy a sandwich,
And toothpaste.
I ache from sleeping on concrete
I am exhausted from being awakened every couple of hours
To be told to move on.
From sleeping with my eyes open waiting
For those who would steal from me
Or do worse.
I am angry at the cruel words thrown at me,
At those who do not even see in me
Another human being, another child of God.
I've already learned the lesson of bitterness
Towards others,
And to live with pain while my body rejects me.
Who is there to help me?
Is this a test, God?
Or is this my life now?

Use this page for notes or make this prayer your own.

The voice of praise is strong and loud
Not meek, nor stuttering.
It commands life with its knowledge
Of I Am.
My voice of praise is Yours,
My God.

Use this page for notes or make this prayer your own.

I am excited
With all the strength in my being,
All the truth of Your words.
My life has been long,
In many places at many times I have stood for
Your redemption
I have fought the fight of compassion,
I have worn the shield of trust
And I have fought with the sword of loving kindness.
It has not been easy
I have skirmished with doubt, struggled with fear
At times I have fallen to my knees, crippled,
And called Your name.
I have always spoken with a voice of trust,
Of loud supplication
Proving You to those who fought beside me,
That they be not discouraged.
I am a warrior for You,
I believe in Your Voice more
Than I believe in my own existence.

My life has been long
And now this warrior is feeble.
But no enemy sword will touch me in my exhaustion
Because I am not exhausted
I am full of joy and excitement.
Today the angels call to me
I get to go home.

Use this page for notes or make this prayer your own.

God, I love You so
My words are not enough
Life itself is not enough
To show my love for You.
God, I love You so.

Use this page for notes or make this prayer your own.

I am distraught, I am disturbed
My body is wracked with pain and my strength is failing
Show me pity, show me mercy
Look with favor upon me;
I can't do this anymore.
Through this pain, teach me how to breathe
In my weakness tell me what to pray
Should I have faith to live, reborn through this pain?
Or should I accept this horror and wait for Your release?
Tell me how to pray, God,
I can't do this anymore.
Teach me to speak softly when I want to rail in anger
To threaten, to beg, to cajole
To ask if You are there.
Where are You, God?
I am crippled in breath, I am broken in movement,
And surely great demons eat my insides!
Be my thoughts because I can no longer think
Through this pain.
Water my bones because I can no longer cry,
There are no tears left, only hopeless darkness.
Hold me, God, give me solace.
Bring me peace;
I can't do this anymore.

Use this page for notes or make this prayer your own.

Like the sun rising over the sea
You cast Your perfect love on me.
Like the sun going down in the west
You cleanse my day and give me rest.

Use this page for notes or make this prayer your own.

I'm losing my family,
I am left alone, and I don't know what to do.
Show me a way out of the trap of my life.
Please, do not leave me to despair,
Loose me from this trap of my own making, God.
Fill my family with love for me again
Fix the wrongs that I have done
Help me see the mistakes I have made,
Bring me understanding.
I am filled with shame, yet
I don't know what I've done wrong
Explain it to me, God,
Help me make amends
Save our family, please, please
Don't let love run out on us.
Where will my wife go, where will my children be?
Who will care for them? Who will care for me?
I am losing my family; save this family, please.

Use this page for notes or make this prayer your own.

Thank you, God, for Your gifts
For quiet whispers
For the safety of resting on You, for
The closets I pray in, for answers
Before I ask.
My praise runneth over.
Thank you God of All.

Use this page for notes or make this prayer your own.

Do not throw me from the garden of Your love
Please do not despise my mistakes
Or my shortcomings.
My ignorance rules me
How will I know what to do?
I don't even know what I know.
I crawl; I can barely stand outside your garden.

Do not throw me from the garden of Your love,
Do not despise me
The way I despise myself
Free me from this fruit of sorrow
Keep my eyes on your mercy
And let my words be only of Thee.

Use this page for notes or make this prayer your own.

Let the world know that I am in service
To the God of omnipotence
To the God of all gods.

Use this page for notes or make this prayer your own.

In the Book of Life, You have written my name.
I have been created by the Author,
A character upon this page.
With a body so I can do
With a mind so I can think
With a mouth so I can speak
Of Your perfection.
With a soul that acknowledges You.
I am written by the Master,
And the Master is written on my heart.

Use this page for notes or make this prayer your own.

I love my toys.
Mommy said You made it possible
For me to have my toys.
My beautiful dollies, my games and my books,
All my stuffed animals and my favorite pony.
Thank You for making it possible.
Not everyone has toys like mine.

Mommy says I have to think like You
Think what You would do before I do anything.
So, I am going to make it possible for other kids
To have nice toys.
I put my dollies, but not all of them,
And my stuffed animals and games and books
In a box and Mommy's going to give it
To kids that weren't possible before.
That's what You did for me.
I hope You like it, God.

Use this page for notes or make this prayer your own.

No voice of an angel can sing Your praise any louder than I
No voice can speak Your word any stronger than I
No heart can love God any better than mine,
You are everything to me.

God, see my heart, and forgive my words.
Let not my love for You show itself
In vain boastfulness.

Use this page for notes or make this prayer your own.

There is a stink so rank, so foul
I despise that I hate to touch it,
I am better than this.
I give to causes
I have two ears and I listen
I laugh and I cry with those I love.
An upright member of society
I do good works,
I stand tall in my beliefs
I put dollars in cups, in hands.
I am better than this.
Make me better than this.

Standing on the corner
Full of grease and filthy clothes
That may never have been washed,
Hair worse than lank; ankles squished out
Of shoes so tight, too small.
I have never seen shoes that tight.
Eyes as dead as hopelessness
Stink so rank, so foul,
I despise that I hate to touch it.
I am better than this. I am godly,
Make me better than this.

Use this page for notes or make this prayer your own.

Great God, I sing for You
I sing for You alone
Let me have perfect pitch
And the voice of angels
To sing a song worthy of You.

Use this page for notes or make this prayer your own.

I visit heaven in my dreams
God is there.
The smile of God is in everything,
The cups of peace overrun,
The surety of Love overwhelms me.
I visit heaven in my dreams.
God is there.

Use this page for notes or make this prayer your own.

The roads diverge, my God
My mind is unable to decide on one.
Where are you, knowledge?
My heart is confused. Which way is my truth?
Which is my best, which is Your will?
God, I do not see You beckoning on the road;
I don't hear You calling to me.
How then can I follow?
Guide my choice;
I cannot find my way.

Use this page for notes or make this prayer your own.

In the meadow I praise You
I am filled with Your wonder and brilliance.
You are the Sun
The voice of the winds,
The strength of the mountains.
You are all that we see
And that which we don't see.
You are the sweet sap hidden in the maple tree
The gold hidden in stone.
You are the thirst-quenching water of a quiet pool
Snowdrops in their season.
You are the Reason for my life.
You are brighter than the brilliant Sun.

Use this page for notes or make this prayer your own.

In hollow-ringing churches and temples I look for You
In the loudest of hallelujahs sitting there,
Your spirit is mostly not.
I seek Your truth in the evangelists and the gifts they request
I do not find You.
I seek Your face in the forests of trees, in the faces of babes,
There You are, my God.
God,
Help me to see You even in hollow
Churches and temples, in empty hallelujahs.

Use this page for notes or make this prayer your own.

I see a shooting star and make a wish
For love, wisdom, and knowledge.
I find a green m&m, and as I eat it I wish
For love, wisdom, and knowledge
Quickly chewing to make the wish come true.
I break a wishbone and I ask
For love, wisdom, and knowledge,
I blow at dandelion fluff and make this my wish.
When I blow away an eyelash, I wish the same.
When my birthday comes, I wish hard
For love, wisdom, and knowledge.
Because You give love, wisdom, and knowledge
And I want even my superstitions and wishes to call
Your Name.

Use this page for notes or make this prayer your own.

Give me counsel, God
I am surrounded by wickedness
In Your house there are deacons who rape little girls
Priests who rape little boys
Men who sacrifice innocence on the altar of not-You.
My governors speak of justice through pointed teeth
While eating the surety You have bequeathed us,
Spitting poison into our waters and
Treading with hooved feet on our dwellings.
Give us strength, God;
Your children rise up in hate
With clubs and weapons, they fall upon each other.
The blood of babies anoints streets
They wet fingers in it and anoint their faces.
The pits of hell have opened upon us
And we cannot tell the difference
God be the lamp of truth in this darkness of souls.

Use this page for notes or make this prayer your own.

You are mighty, You are true
I will always recognize You
You are mighty, You are true
You are the purpose in all that I do.

Use this page for notes or make this prayer your own.

Thank you, God of Everything
For being my breath this morning
For sight and sound
And the beat of my heart
For the start of a blessed day
Thank you, my Everything.

Use this page for notes or make this prayer your own.

I've lost my patience today.
The world around me is driving me crazy
I can't do everything
I can't deal with questions and demands
I can't stand judgement by those who do not know me.
Show me mercy, give me patience
That I can pass on.

Use this page for notes or make this prayer your own.

In these thousands of years, the lamps have become dim
The batteries drained
Faith has become a word on the tongue.
I am lost in the dark, evil surrounds me
Please blind me with Your light.

O, God, my teacher
Whose word is great
My questions are also great.
In whispers I have asked of Thee
In tears I have begged Thee
In great shouts I have demanded of Thee
Never once believing in Your silence.

But in the words of my youth, I questioned Your presence.
With murmurs of doubt and ultimatums,
Too busy with my questions to hear answers.
Now that I know Your voice
Now that I recognize Your voice
Where are Your answers?

Use this page for notes or make this prayer your own.

I forgot Your name today
I tried to remember.
I tried to remember
But Your name eluded me.
I have forgotten those around me
I have forgotten love, where did it go?
I do not remember pretty pictures
Or sad-looking faces.
I forget what food I like, and which
Is my right and left;
I cannot find the bathroom.

I forgot my name yesterday
And the day before
But You knew me before birth
Before I was born You held me in Your love.
You knew my soul before I existed.
I am frightened that I forgot.
How can I forget You?
Is it a sin?
Please whisper my name
So I remember,
And hold me tight
When I don't remember.

Use this page for notes or make this prayer your own.

Everything, You are my Everything
You are my awaking
You are my daytime and my sleeping
I am set in Your ways
And I walk in Your footsteps.

Use this page for notes or make this prayer your own.

As the river runs to the ocean
So does my heart run to You.
As the bird rises upward
So do my hands raise to You.
As the sun creates fire
So am I on fire for You.
As the great stones stand fast
I stand fast in You.
I stand fast in You.

Use this page for notes or make this prayer your own.

It's hard to take another step,
Each one is methodical, excruciating
There is no smile to be found to offer another on the path.
Breathing is slow
And my thoughts ask: why bother?
Who could hold my weight if I lean on them?
Who will put aside his own needs to listen to mine,
Again and again?
There is no one.
I will go home and alone
Cry giant screaming tears into my nakedness
Until I throw up pain and can neither see nor breathe.
Then, though I can't see You and I don't hear You
I will grab hold of You, my God
And live another night.

Use this page for notes or make this prayer your own.

Can You see me, God?
Has some dark spell made me invisible?
Have I disappeared from Your presence?
Am I walking alone?
Find me, my God.
I am lost.

Use this page for notes or make this prayer your own.

I am slow, but I am steady
I stop too often to ask the way,
But the way is important to me.
Others become impatient
But You are important to me;
You are the way.
I pray without ceasing.
I sing Your music badly
But I sing it with love which makes it beautiful to me.
I stand and sway to music others cannot hear.
I dance with the angels.
My thoughts are not always clear
So I stop and ask direction
Which You give to me.

Use this page for notes or make this prayer your own.

In Your Name, I will lift my brother and carry him
When he has fallen on the road.
I will stop to give him drink when he thirsts,
And bread when he hungers.
I will spare him change when he begs on the street
I will pray with him.
Is that enough?
Must I do this when he is not my brother?
When his church is not mine?
When it is not easy, and I am put out?
When he is full of booze,
And his body is filled with drugs?
When his body is no longer filled with drugs,
And he is hostile
Or dangerous?
When he is a psychopath?
When do I lift him up or pray with him?
Is it enough just to pray for him as I continue on?
When I do not want to touch him
When she is an intrusion
When it will take my life
Speak to me so I hear You, speak
So I understand.
What does my faith require?

Use this page for notes or make this prayer your own.

When I was a babe
Resting on horsehair pews
I did not know Your word, but I knew You,
Who surrounded me with a blanket of angels.
When I was a child in a hate filled world
Somewhere people prayed for me
And I felt Your love protect me.
When I was filled with an unclear mind
And the torments of crazy
I held to Your hand
As if it were the only thing to save me.
When I became an adult
I thanked You in good times
And praised You in terrible times
I praised You in faith
Which was the only thing I had.
When I felt no immediacy of answer,
I still praised You.
It is the only thing I can do because we promised each other
It's You and me 'til the wheels fall off.

Use this page for notes or make this prayer your own.

.

We will sing with our voices
Play Your praise on the piano
On the guitar, on the drums.
Together we will sing
Songs of trust in You,
Songs of praise to You.

For You are the light of the world,
The honey on our tongues
The answer to our prayers.
You are the truth on which we build our lives,
The answer to our prayers.

Use this page for notes or make this prayer your own.

I have stood alone in the dark
I have fasted, and I have prayed
For Your lamp to light my way
For understanding to manifest in me
Speak to me God, that I may hear You.

Use this page for notes or make this prayer your own.

I never knew it could be like this
Without fear, concern and worry
Without something peering out to distract me
To make false my witness.
I never knew it could be like this.
Your grace shooting throughout my being
My everything in Your hands
This is what knowing is.
My whole body feels electric
My heart is so full I cannot stop crying
I cannot stop crying
I cannot stop rocking
I cannot stop praising Your name.
This taste of heaven will keep me longing for home.
I never knew it could be like this.

Use this page for notes or make this prayer your own.

I'm unbalanced, and I'm devastated
I am cut and cauterized,
Unwhole and I will never be the same.
Unwhole, unwhole
What has been given has been taken
A tiny lump the size of a pea
Has taken my womanhood from me.
How can there be only a scar,
When I can feel it there?
How will I suckle a child,
Without fearing she may be drinking
The tainted milk of my sickness?
How can I know the illness is gone?
How can I live with the fear
That one day the whole of my womanhood will be gone?
That I will never be able to suckle
That my chest will become scarred and flat?
Then I will no longer be a woman.
My Fear is a high mountain
Remove my fear, dear God.

Use this page for notes or make this prayer your own.

On treacherous roads I walk
Sharp stones cut my feet
Straight cliffs fill my vision.
I am scared
I am lonely
But I am determined to walk Your path.

Use this page for notes or make this prayer your own.

.

Let my prayers be Holy, Holy
Let my prayers be Alleluia,
I have no words for Your majesty
I have no words for Your glory,
I must borrow them.
May these words in my heart be magnified
By the love I have for You.
My heart explodes with Your magnificence.

Use this page for notes or make this prayer your own.

I sing You my gratitude
I sing Your works of love.
I sing with beating heart, with every blade of grass
With the leaves on the trees
And the wind on high.
I sing to You of gratitude
With every bird that flies
With each mountain and each grain of sand
My voice is joined with all of Creation
With the very stars in the sky.

Use this page for notes or make this prayer your own.

There's so much I want, God
So many things to bless this life.
I could count them to you
But before any number must be this:
You. I want You.
I want to be closer, closest, as close as I can be to
Your presence
And many other things, but this above all
Make me One with You.
From youth up, this has been my prayer
Above all, before all, in All
Make me One with You.
Read my soul, see my tears of earnestness
Try my heart to see if I am lying.
I need You like I need to breathe
More than I need to breathe.
Many other things, but You above all.

Use this page for notes or make this prayer your own.

Getting older, getter slower
Getting deafer, getting blinder.
Becoming solo
As those around me pass away
Like leaves falling from the trees
In the autumn of, the winter of
Their lives.
Getting older, getting frailer
Becoming obsolete
Disrespected like a child
Called 'dearie', 'honey', 'sweetie',
Patted by hands taking liberties
Hands I do not know.
They have no intimacy to have the right
To behave like that.
Getting older, getting less patient
With my small world around me
Trying me every day;
I attempt to be kind
Because I think they would treat me better if they knew
That I am going home soon, and there I will be
Hand in hand with God.

Use this page for notes or make this prayer your own.

I can't touch you
I can't look at you,
But I can think about you
In this world in which I live.
I might make some movements that you don't understand.
I might need something to focus my hands
And focus my thoughts, because
My brain is so full of everything and nothing.
I might move fast, or I might be slow,
But my brain is whirring in a world you don't know,
Too, too busy,
And your touch makes it too much.
Don't be fooled; God knows what He's doing
He made me like this:
Rare and special.
You won't understand me, and that's all right
But when you pray for me in your bed at night
I hear you, and God hears you, too.

Use this page for notes or make this prayer your own.

Fire has its own life,
Merciless and grasping,
No respecter of persons.
Fire races through buildings,
Up walls
Into bodies.
Nothing escapes.

We are the enemies of fire.
We understand its ways,
Know its soul.
We are warriors in uniform
Impeding the escape of fire,
Entering its very heart,
Striking it dead.
We claim Your protection
Greatest God,
Give our crew Your Breath of Life
When fire tries to steal ours.

Use this page for notes or make this prayer your own.

Share the word of God
Make a present of God's love
Espouse His omnipotence
And His faithfulness.

Share the love of God
To all you meet, in all you do
Shine brightly so all may say:
What has her?

Share the victory of God
Reach with love for those in need
Help them to rise
Through your acceptance.

They will ask, what has him?
We will say:
It is God.

Use this page for notes or make this prayer your own.

Thank You for the circle of friends around me,
For their love and caring
For the support they give daily
I feel You in them.
Thank You for my friends
Who I love,
Support and care about.
We are strong together.
Thank You for our strength.
Thank You for us.
I pray for us,
That love takes our hearts
That our choices may be wise
And our endeavors successful
Walk each step with us.
Guide me to be a good friend
Help me shine for them.

Use this page for notes or make this prayer your own.

When I'm scared, I call Your name
When I feel joy, I do the same.

When I wake or when I rest
I live in You who love me best;
When I stay still or when I move
I worship God whose name is Love.
And when at night I'm on my knees
I praise my God who brings me peace.

Use this page for notes or make this prayer your own.

What can I believe, God,
When You let these things happen?
Babies with heads bashed against walls
Buried, drowned, thrown in dumpsters
Thrown out windows?
Toddlers shooting toddlers.
Most of them will not know You,
Will they go to heaven?

What can I believe, God
When bullying and cyberbullying are the
Normal responses of playground playmates?
When vitriolic words are spit like acid?
When there is hate in the religion of love?
When man does not believe You created man
All men, in Your own image.
When peoples around the world have not known You
Before they die
Will they go to heaven?
What can I believe, God?

Use this page for notes or make this prayer your own.

For every square foot
And every room on every floor,
For the inside and the out
We give thanks.

For the corners and the ceilings
For plumbing and electricity,
For carpets and floors
We give thanks.

For good schools and good neighbors
For all amenities,
For this new home You've blessed us with
We give thanks.

Use this page for notes or make this prayer your own.

When I rise up, then I fall down,
Help me pick myself from the ground.
You are my strength, God.

When things get hard, and I become angry,
Please come nigh and give patience to me.
You are my protector, God.

When life is upsetting, and I get depressed,
Bring solace to me and give me rest.
You are my Counselor, God.

When I feel the Spirit, and my hands I raise,
All I can do is give You praise,
You are my Blessed God.

Use this page for notes or make this prayer your own.

I have a ministry, God, I have a purpose,
To lead Your sheep,
To counsel Your children, believers,
In Your way.
To educate, to keep them on the path.
I have a purpose, God, and it is Your purpose.
Do You think they know that sometimes I feel
So far from You,
Sometimes I'm just doing the best I can
Because I don't know what I'm doing?
I think some of them don't know I'm
Only human.
Please help me, God, to know Your will;
Help me to lead with authority,
To walk Your path with joy,
To teach others to walk Your path.
Help me inspire, help me to be a blessing
Help me do Your will to the best of my ability.
In thy Name,
Amen.

Use this page for notes or make this prayer your own.

I struggled not to know You,
Not to see You, not to hear You,
When You came to me.
I planned to live all by myself,
No words of interference,
No one to tell me what to do.
I made my own decisions
Took responsibility
Traveled my own highway.
Now life has become tangled
String upon string, all in knots;
I am obliged to ask for help.
I was a proud man, without humility
But pride goeth before a fall,
And how the mighty are fallen!
I humbly ask of You
To come to me again.
This time I will listen.

Use this page for notes or make this prayer your own.

In the beginning was the Word.
And the Word spoke in my ear:
Walk with Me; be Mine
Have no other god before Me,
And if you are faithful to Me
I will bless you all the days of your life.

I am old now,
I have walked with God,
I have been His, and His alone.
I have been faithful to Him,
And He has been with me;
He has blessed me all these days of my life.

Use this page for notes or make this prayer your own.

An army of angels is with me.
I stand firm in place
In my prayer, in God's name
At the crossroads.

Four roads are before me.
Three roads do not serve me
In God's will, in my duty.
I stand at the crossroads.

An army of angels to guide me
Protect me from temptation,
Because I have chosen God's way
Before ever I stopped at these crossroads.

The crossroads of decision
Is never simple or easy
It is commitment and sacrifice,
I have an army of angels at the crossroads.

Use this page for notes or make this prayer your own.

Is this Your doing, Your ending for us?
Our country is in chaos, and I am frightened
Brothers killing brothers, and mothers, and wives
Color against color
Faith against faith
While our leaders, with glossy smiles
Egg them on.
Weapons or no weapons
Poisons and fists
Anger and hatred and vicious words
From true believers.
War after war for thousands of years
We face nuclear bombs
While our leaders serve only themselves
To generous helpings
Of our survival.
Is this our end? Do we all die?
I have faith in You
But is it really faith if I'm afraid?

Use this page for notes or make this prayer your own.

My trust is in You, O God
As I climb the mountains, as I descend the valleys
My trust is in You
When men don't understand me
While they laugh and mock me
My trust is in You.
When the waters engulf me,
When the sharks circle me
My trust is in You.

Use this page for notes or make this prayer your own.

We have come to celebrate
The union of these hearts
Two souls brought up in love
Attaining love.
They have chosen one another
Promised one another life with one another.
In Your sight,
They request Your blessing
Heads bowed, hand in hand.
We have come to watch these two people
Become one in Your love.
We have come to offer hands and hearts and prayers
For Your blessings in their lives,
As this couple leaves together
To become one in their new life.

Use this page for notes or make this prayer your own.

Make me in Your image, God,
Let me walk within Your footsteps.
Make my thoughts pure
My speech without judgement
My heart speaking love.
Make me in Your image, God.
Let me see through Your eyes
Help me listen compassionately,
Let me hear what is not said.
May my hands joyfully do Your work
Let my smile be soft and loving
Let Your life-light shine through me.

Use this page for notes or make this prayer your own.

Thank You, thank You,
Your love endures forever.
Thank You, thank You,
Your mercy forgives us forever.
Thank You, thank You,
Your strength protects us forever.
Thank You, thank You,
I will praise Your name forever.

Use this page for notes or make this prayer your own.

I am so happy in You!
God,
You are the fullness of me;
I am possessed.
I cry Hallelujah, and I speak in the tongues of angels,
Your name is forever on my lips.
My cup runneth over with joy,
My arms are lifted, and my hands reach to You.
I have heard Your word and been blessed.
I stand in the presence of the faithful.
I sing Hallelujah to You
My face shines with love for You
May it ever be so.

Use this page for notes or make this prayer your own.

I claim Your promises in this unknown country
Where we face the unfamiliar,
Where what is similar is still fearful
I claim Your protection in this horrific situation
For myself and my platoon.
I know Your promises are good.
Your angels surround us,
Your protection encompasses us
We believe You, we believe in You.
We are Yours
And none shall harm us.
Amen.

Use this page for notes or make this prayer your own.

How grateful I am
To the Highest of the High
God, how full is my heart.
I am Joyous
For you have provided me
The perfection of a partner.
Our hands fit
Our kisses are sacred
Our thoughts are joined.
How grateful I am.

Use this page for notes or make this prayer your own.

I love You, God.
It's as simple as that.
If there were no love,
No praise,
No blessings surrounding me
To lead me to You,
If life hid You from me,
Made me blind and deaf and
Unable to move,
I would still know You were there
And I would still call upon Your name.

Use this page for notes or make this prayer your own.

In this war, do I have a choice?
How shall I answer Your commandments?
I have honored my father and mother,
I have not committed adultery,
I have had no other god before Thee,
I have not yet killed;
I shalt not war.
How do I respond to this
Terrible decision that seals my guilt?
How shall I fight?
How do I shalt not kill?
In my eyes I see bodies under foot
Blood running down my body
My enemies and my brothers
Pierced by bullets of hate and righteousness.
Guide me,
For my eyes are swollen with crying
I cannot see the way in my confusion.
Please let my choices be Yours
How shall I not war?

Use this page for notes or make this prayer your own.

Not one friend's face I'll evermore see,
No laughing, no hugging, no being together
No whispers of support,
The kind I had before.
Strange town
Strange house,
Strange people.
So much strangeness makes me uneasy.
I'm unsure of myself,
And my standing
With these people.
Will I wear the right clothes?
Will I say the right words?
Will I meet the right kids who will be my friends?
How will I know them?
I hate this town of unknown
I miss my friends
And I am uncertain.
God, take my hand, and be my friend.

Use this page for notes or make this prayer your own.

Here am I
On my knees before You,
Seeking reassurance from that still, small voice.
What am I going to do?
My assurance is gone. My confidence is gone.
What am I going to do?
After all my faithful service
I have been rejected, I have been let go.
I am trying so hard,
But I feel like nothing, useless,
How shall I provide? How will I pay my bills
Without money coming in?
What if no one wants me?
What new skills must I learn to compete?
I am bereft
How will we survive?
Here I am on my knees today, asking You for answers.

Use this page for notes or make this prayer your own.

When a leaf falls from a very tall tree
And lands in a pile of a hundred other leaves
You know which one it is.
When a star explodes, one star in a
Universe of Universes of stars
You know which star it is.
When my voice seeks You
Through a billion other voices
Chattering, laughing, crying,
Praying,
You know which voice mine is.
Truly You are God.

Use this page for notes or make this prayer your own.

How did You arrange it, God?
How did You work it that we fit so well?
My hand in his hand,
My thoughts with his,
Our prayers together.
Surely, God,
The love we have for each other
Is in You.

Use this page for notes or make this prayer your own.

I believe in You, truly I do
Yet I don't have confidence in Your promises.
What if I put my faith in You
Will You pay my bills?
Bring me what I desire?
Keep my health?
Will I have to give up everything?
Are You going to take everything from me?
I believe in You,
But You are so far away
So separate.
I must work hard
To keep myself,
And protect my money.
But what I secretly want of You,
In case You disapprove,
Is when I worship You on Sunday
You won't notice the rest.

Use this page for notes or make this prayer your own.

Kill me now, please.
Don't make me live another day
In hallucinations
In terror of falling down the rabbit hole
In ultimate fear, in total separation.
No one else understands
No one will understand,
It's a secret club
Only open to members who've been there.
Our own special club they can't comprehend.
Please kill me now.
Or release me from hell
From this pit so wide I can't find the sides
So deep I can't see the sun
From the hopelessness
Of feeling it has always been like this,
And ever will be.
I beg You to kill me now.
I can't remember if You exist; I can't see You,
I can't hear You
If you do exist, break my heart, stroke me out
Let me get hit by a train.
I can't stand this pain,
I beg You, God, please kill me now.

Use this page for notes or make this prayer your own.

As I stand in this empty house today
And each person enters I pray,
Let them see in this house a home
Let them feel all the love sown
In each nook and every space;
Know this is the perfect place
For one very special one
Who will make of it a home.

Use this page for notes or make this prayer your own.

Walk with me, talk with me, be every breath I breathe,
Show me Your footsteps and I will follow You.
Let me hear Your voice
In the raging winds and the calm moments
And I will obey Your word.
Let the breath of Life enter my body
And my words will sound Your glory
And I will speak of the love of my God forever.

Use this page for notes or make this prayer your own.

And fat men with their packed camels could not go
Through that mountain pass
Without first releasing their burdens.
In the same way am I joyful
In what You have given me
But I do not choose any of this more than You.
I unburden myself of my desires
And walk easily through the eye of the Needle.
One cannot love God and love things equally,
I shall have no other gods before me.
There is only You for me.
You are my security.

Use this page for notes or make this prayer your own.

As I lay me down to rest,
My head hangs down upon my chest
This deep sleep is borne of drink; make me sober ere I wake.
I can drink one or maybe another,
I am always in control
Except those days, those nights, those hours
When I can't remember what I've done.
Have I wet myself, have I caused a fire,
Have I killed a valued friendship?
Did I run a light, did I crash my car,
Did I kill someone, was there damage done?
Did I finally push away my beloved?
Did I get fired, did I get in a fight,
Make midnight calls, or call all night,
Did I drink up all my rent?
Did I forget my kids in the store,
To feed them or clothe them, did I show them the door?
Did the authorities remove my children?
I can drink one, and maybe another
I'm always the life of the party
I laugh and I laugh, then I cry and I cry
Or somebody starts a fight by and by
Something always crashes, and someone always burns,
And someone always makes love to the cool porcelain.
Sometimes it's me and sometimes it's not,
I just can't remember what yesterday brought.
It's fun to be flirting, did I take it too far?
Did I threaten or beg or cajole?
Was I laying in puke, was I laying in sin
It's not as much fun as I thought it would be
Like having a devil hanging off me
The one in control is the drink.
I'm in hell when I try to stop
When I try to shut it off,
Then the devil offers me another one.
Help me to help myself, God.

Use this page for notes or make this prayer your own.

The job was good, God,
I was doing well.
Then came the injury,
And the extended time out of work.
The drugs,
The huge medical bills,
And more.
I'm leaning on You, God,
I'm looking for the door You've opened
Since You closed this one
When I lost my job.
I can't work;
I can hardly move without crying
And the bills keep coming in.
Medical bills,
Living expenses;
I can't afford to pay for insurance
Which I need;
I can either pay for medicine
Or feed my family.
It's a lose/lose situation
These days, God
There's nothing I can do
I'm helpless and I'm starting
To feel hopeless.
It's been so long.
I'm waiting for that door to open
I've been praying, and I need help
I need it right now.
I know there's a way
Open my eyes to see it,
Give me courage to follow it
I'm still trusting You.

Use this page for notes or make this prayer your own.

For Your perfection I bow before You
For Your faithfulness I bow before You
For Your unconditional love I bow before You
I bow before my God.

Use this page for notes or make this prayer your own.

Is she with You now?
I pray that's the case.
We can't find her here
In this hospital bed
In this broken body.
We pray for her every hour
We visit her every day
We speak to her
Ask her and beg her
But we can't find her in here.
Her body is healing each day
But they've decided she never will.
If she's with You
We beg of You to return her to us.
Is she lying here stuck in her mind?
Is she wandering out in the ether?
We don't know if she's there with You
Just that we can't find her in here.
They say that she's every bit dead
That she'll never return here to us,
That her organs will bless others in need
But is she dead just because we can't see?
It's been so long.
Can You please let us know what to do?
We can pull the plug if we know she's with You
We need Your word to help us get through
Because we can't find her in here.

Use this page for notes or make this prayer your own.

Dear God, see this child today
Broken bones and bruises,
A stoic child, quick to say
He fell when he went out to play
None of us believe it.
Look at his file, look how full,
He's been here so many times
Another contusion, another break,
How many more times will it take
Till he comes back to die?
Help me God, to know what to say
That will make a difference to them today
To take this fearful family
Away from the monster we all see
To help them get away.

God, my heart bleeds; I am asking You,
You could have stopped this, but what did You do?
He killed his only son
Whose life is over before it begun
A beautiful child who had never done wrong
A few short years, then he was gone
Never more to live or play
But never another pain-filled day.
He'd be alive if You stopped this man
Am I supposed to believe this was Your plan?

Use this page for notes or make this prayer your own.

I am done, we are ended.
I can't even recall the love that began us
The passion and touching, the feelings
The love we promised in Your name.
He no longer makes me feel wanted
And I no longer make him feel strong
I don't know how it slipped away
Or where it went, or how we got here,
There is both an absence and a pain in my heart
In my body, in my life.
I know he feels the same.
We have acrimony, we have anger and fear,
We have judgement.
There is nothing in this that is Your love
No hiding place I hold You.
I want to love him, but I do not.
I want Your love to heal us of this.
I'm asking for both of us –
Return to us the love we do not feel.

Use this page for notes or make this prayer your own.

In my distress
The rocks call out
The birds sing
The very earth resounds
With a booming bass of
Alleluia.
And I am comforted.

Use this page for notes or make this prayer your own.

When did You do this, my God?
When did You have your way with me
When You opened my eyes
And cleared my ears
When Your word settled into my heart?
I bless You, my God.

Use this page for notes or make this prayer your own.

This feels too good to let it go,
Yet it forces me into anxiety and desperation,
Guilt and fear and pain.
I am chained by my desire,
Tormented by my very own demon,
There is no freedom.
When I try to leave, I am pulled back
By uncontrolled, violent shaking,
By unseen imps crawling painfully under my skin,
By convulsive, gut tearing vomiting,
By shrill screaming and interminable banging inside my head,
By the cold of ice, the heat of hell enveloping me,
By voices, voices, voices,
Talking to me, directing me, commanding me
Holding me hostage, forcing me,
Dragging me back to the dreams of drugs
Again, and again,
Until I need more.
I don't know what time it is, what day it is
I don't know where my friends are,
Who my friends are.
And how can I possibly manage my day?
The demon has exhausted me. There is no escape.
I have heard of You, God,
Will You free me from my prison,
Will You cut my bonds and vanquish my demon jailor?
I beg You to free me from the chains of hell.
Free me and I will praise You evermore.

Use this page for notes or make this prayer your own.

My heart is breaking,
Have I not been a good servant to You?
Have I not followed Your path and kept Your words?
Why have You turned Your face from me?
Why have You turned Your back on me?
Where are You now?
Do not imprison me in lack of love
Don't turn away from me, God
Have mercy on Your servant.

Use this page for notes or make this prayer your own.

If You say jump, my God,
I'll not ask how high.
I'll follow You until I die
I'll walk on water though I drown
I'll jump off cliffs though I fall down
I'll walk in fire though I burn
I'll do all these things with no concern,
For I walk in faith and I walk in love
Trusting in the God above
When my God's voice compels me to;
Whatever You ask, that will I do.

Use this page for notes or make this prayer your own.

When I was a babe in my innocence
There was never a reason to doubt.
You didn't tell anyone,
But around every corner I saw You.

When I was a child in Your house
Where they sang, they prayed, and they read,
They spoke of seeing by faith.
In every face there, I saw You.

When I was a teenager in the church
They worried that I might chose to leave You.
I was never concerned by their doubts,
They never knew that I saw You.

Now that I see You in faith,
I feel closer than ever to You
I love You ever the more all because
You showed Yourself, and I saw You.

Use this page for notes or make this prayer your own.

I am thankful for this farm and all the good things it brings,
Thankful for the abundance of its bounty.
My fields are full of corn this year
My cows are producing,
The hens are giving eggs
In such abundance we can share.

My children have new clothes to wear,
Our bills are being paid
And we have meat on the table.
No storms nor blights, the crops are growing high
I thank You for this farm and all its bounty
For the good You have blessed us with this year.

Use this page for notes or make this prayer your own.

Thank You, my Everything
Thank You for being my breath this morning,
Thank You for sight and sound
And the beat of my heart.
Thank You for the start of a blessed day.
Thank You, my Everything.

Use this page for notes or make this prayer your own.

I come to You, my God
For I have found a man who has become my husband,
And I have inherited his children
Who I think of as my children
They have taken my heart to a special place.
Help me to win their hearts
Not to compete, nor to compare
But to complement.
Help me to show them my love
Unconditionally.
Limitless, immeasurable
That they may see Your love
Shining through me.

Use this page for notes or make this prayer your own.

You are with me God
No matter where I am, there You are.
When I speak with my enemies,
When I face my detractors,
When I look at those I love,
You are there.
You are my life,
You direct the work of my hands.
Even my smile belongs to You.

Use this page for notes or make this prayer your own.

God, when I see people at their worst
I don't know how You do it.
They come in here
With their immediacy, their illness and pain,
Sometimes turning to anger.
They are needy
They do not want to follow the production line
Of requirements
Before seeing someone who may not understand their needs.
I am the one who listens,
The professional hand-holder.

When I see people at their worst
I smile and speak with confidence
Call them by name,
And listen
Through their pain and anger.
I don't know how You can listen to all the pain of the world
While I only hear these few
And feel their desperation.
Help me to help them, to show them Your love,
Because for some, I am the only You they have.

Use this page for notes or make this prayer your own.

Neither snow nor rain nor heat
Nor gloom of night will stay Your follower
From the swift completion of Your will.

Use this page for notes or make this prayer your own.

We give You thanks before we say congratulations
For You are the provider of all good things in life.
We bless the good of our companion
We share her joy,
And it is good –
You are the provider of all good things.

Use this page for notes or make this prayer your own.

Forgive me, God, for believing
That food is more powerful than You,
That even though You are the Omnipotent Creator of All
I believe I can't be saved from this demon.
I dieted
I 'watched my weight' as it rose
I have been subjected to the judgement of others
Speaking quietly or sometimes loudly,
Deriding, laughing
Saying:
Have some control,
What a pig,
You'd be pretty if;
I am a failure.
Do they think I want to be like this?
That I do not want to have strength,
Or love for my body?
I reached out to You
I claimed in Your name
I cried to You, begged You
But no changes came.
What do I do?
Am I a failure even in Your eyes?
I do not hear Your answer.
I am in pain, both body and soul,
My weight makes me too tired to live this life.
I am desperate,
What must I do to gain Your help?

Use this page for notes or make this prayer your own.

.

God:
When I choose Your ways
Choose Your will
Open to understanding
Pray for Your guidance
Show thankfulness and thoughtfulness
I have peace.

Use this page for notes or make this prayer your own.

I have chosen this moment to pray.
In the perfection of the calm sea,
Bright sun, blue sky;
I smell salted water
All is in rightness.
Alone with God
I have chosen this moment to pray.
My prayers swell like the swell of the ocean
My prayers sparkle like sun on sea
My prayers are clear and calm
Like the blue skies surrounding me;
I have chosen this moment to pray.
And my praise leaps from my lips
Like great creatures the sea cannot contain,
Like seabirds winging to heaven
Does my praise raise.
For here I see God
And I have chosen this moment to pray.

Use this page for notes or make this prayer your own.

I cannot change anyone else, only myself,
I cannot change myself without Your help, God
Guide me, please.
Help me to stop my complaining, intolerance, my anger.
Let me shower my lover with patience and the soothing drops
Of gentle words.
Help me recognize the joy in our beginning,
Help me remember the person with whom I fell in love.
Remove from me my argumentative spirit
Teach me to listen attentively,
Help me to praise, to build-up,
Help me change my negative spirit,
Help me submit to Your will.

Use this page for notes or make this prayer your own.

Creator of everything
I am an unformed slab
On the wheel of this life
Only the clay.
You are the potter
Greatest Master of all
Maker of universes and atoms.
Mold me after Your vision
With the strength of Your will
And the power of Your love.

Use this page for notes or make this prayer your own.

I will speak of Your love forever
I will follow every word
I will speak of Your love forever
Until each and every soul has heard.

Use this page for notes or make this prayer your own.

This house is the Lord's
Bless all who enter here,
Share our love and cheer.
Drop your sorrow and your swords
For this house is the Lord's.

Use this page for notes or make this prayer your own.

He comes home drunk.
She comes to work in sunglasses and long sleeves,
She will hear no words against him.
He is loud and aggressive.
She is quiet and invisible.
She hides in her spirit in case he finds her.
The breaks and the bruises are not nearly as painful
As the razor-sharp words cutting her.
She is a bad person, a nothing, a no one.
She tries so hard to avoid his wrath,
But if not her, then her children.
She protects them with her life, yet
She will hear no words against him.
She does not listen when we approach her
With our prayers for her,
Knowing that one day soon she may die.
We have come together
To pray for Your intercession.
Speak to her, God, maybe she will listen to You.

Use this page for notes or make this prayer your own.

I need more time, God
I haven't said what needs to be said,
I haven't touched him enough,
I haven't told him I forgive him,
Or asked him for forgiveness.
I haven't come to terms with my pain,
I haven't relieved his pain.

My father is dying, dear God
And I am not ready. We need more time,
Time to discuss our history
Time to discuss You,
Time to say good-bye.

Or time to seek a miracle.
I want him here with me
And I will give You anything
Anything at all

To perform a miracle.
I know You can, I beg that You will
I will give You anything
Anything at all.

Let him rise from his bed and walk
Let his days be increased.
I need more time
With my father, God.
Let me have more days of normalcy,
I can't stand his pain,
I can't stand my sorrow,
I can't stand Your silence,
Give us more time together.

Use this page for notes or make this prayer your own.

I wish they could be me for a minute or two
And they'd find out it isn't as easy to focus as everyone says.
Too many things are going on
I get distracted.
I can't sit still; my body is jumpy
It's got to move, and I can't stop it.
I can't focus on numbers and letters
I just can't concentrate;
I've got to be up; I've got to be moving.
I can't stand those kids,
Even my friends
Their voices rattling in my head
Them getting too close
And saying the wrong things.
God, please make me quiet
Help me to concentrate
I can't help it; I don't mean to misbehave
They don't understand.
I can't stop it by myself.
I need your superpower, God,
Please help me.

Use this page for notes or make this prayer your own.

Rise, and speak your truth
Sing your song to the Lord,
Testify.

The Lord is our perfection
The beginning and the end,
The east to the west,
Testify of Him.

The Lord is everywhere present
Who hears and answers prayers,
Who delivers us from our enemies,
And ourselves.
Testify to Him.

Use this page for notes or make this prayer your own.

When he looks at me, I see love shining out,
Each wag of his tail says the same.
He wags his whole body, this waggy-tailed dog.
He exalts in my arrival, is devastated by my leaving
He is happy and content in my presence.
He licks and tricks to make me happy
To earn my praise, to request my touch.
He curls himself into me and sleeps a peaceful sleep.
He protects me from my enemies
And trusts every move I make.

What a gift this dear friend is
Teaching me what unconditional love looks like,
Teaching me patience,
Teaching me to think of others,
In ways I never have.
Truly he is a gift from God.

Use this page for notes or make this prayer your own.

You are the exquisite Maker of All Creation
Yet I don't want to see You now.
I believe in You, but I don't want to leave.

I'm not ready to be sick
I'm not ready to be lying here,
With wires and tubes coming out of me.
I'm not ready for nurses, for doctors
For machines talking around me.

I'm especially not ready for the gurney
Or the operation,
When I will be here with one breath
And somewhere else with the next one,
Not knowing if I'll awake here or in heaven.
I don't want to go to heaven
Not now.
I don't want to die.

Use this page for notes or make this prayer your own.

I've been reading about music and mathematics
How they are the same
In their differentness.
I've been studying physics and God
And here You are
In no thing, in all things.
I've been reading about the universe and spirituality
When my eyes are open I see You.
I see You in the small things and the large things,
In the before and the after
In the up and the down
Surely You are a great God.

Use this page for notes or make this prayer your own.

Bless me God, for I have sinned.
Have mercy in my sorrow
Have forgiveness in my repentance.

Use this page for notes or make this prayer your own.

On the mountains' edge
The bridge is out yet God says "Come,
Have faith in Me
Walk upon My truth.
Open your eyes,
See that I have provided for you.
My word is truth and again I say come."
I am terrified, but I walk,
Carefully putting one foot before another.
And God is with me.

Use this page for notes or make this prayer your own.

Please accept this child
Bring to her Your love
Bring her life to fruition
In Your awareness.
Make us bearers of Your love
As we raise her in Your ways
Guide us as we parent.

Bring her godparents wisdom
To direct her ways
To give her advice and solace.

Bring our child Your strength
As we bring her to You.
Amen.

Use this page for notes or make this prayer your own.

I am blessed, God,
At the top of the mountain
With the woman I love
Blessed with children
Secure in my career
With a multitude of friends.
I have my health,
And a beautiful house with a garage and cars
And money and investments.

I'm on the mountaintop, God
Content in my life.
But You may ask it from me.
If I lose these, what will I have?
I will have You. I will have everything.

Use this page for notes or make this prayer your own.

The name of the God is peace
The face of the God is love
The works of the God are miraculous
The words of the God are pure.

Use this page for notes or make this prayer your own.

My eyes are blind, but I see You, God
I see You in the darkness,
In bursts of glory,
In the brightness of Your presence.
I see You standing, arms outstretched to me.
Although I am blind, I am not blind to You, God.

Use this page for notes or make this prayer your own.

God, I thank You
For You are in my heart
In this muscle
In these tissues
In my cells.
In the atoms
In the infinitesimal quarks.
You are the tiniest pieces of the forever me.

Use this page for notes or make this prayer your own.

God,
We have been trained to be servants
As we walk before men.
We have been trained to serve,
Trained to act without fear
As we enter the shadows.
As we behold confusion, anger, or violence,
Let each step taken
Be in step with You
May each word spoken
Bring peace with it.
May each action be the action of a servant.
Keep us, God, as we go forth
Keep us humble, keep us true to the blue
Save us from pride, greed, and prejudice.
Keep us alive and keep us safe,
As we put on our badges of service
To enter another day.

Use this page for notes or make this prayer your own.

I am nothing, I am less than nothing
In this life, in this universe, in this great Creation
My life is as small as an insect, an ant
Yet You have a plan for me.
Let me be of use to You,
Let me stand before You,
Or allow me only to lay at my Master's feet,
As You will, God.
So I can say I am
Your humble servant.

Use this page for notes or make this prayer your own.

Lying in the desert, I close my eyes
Fly through the universe
Between stars and asteroids.
In the cold, perfect silence there comes singing.
Creation songs
Awakening songs
The universe itself is rumbling with song,
Stars twinkling with song
Planets dancing in song,
Harmonizing with angels.
Lying in the desert, I am filled with song,
I join the angels and sing praise.

Use this page for notes or make this prayer your own.

In the brightness of the rising sun
At the ending of each day
In all things You are my God
I praise Your name.

Use this page for notes or make this prayer your own.

The morning birds sing Glory
Alleluia then rises in morning Glory
Petals and grasses and leaves
Raise their faces to Glory.
Animals of the earth, and all life
Awaken to Glory.
I speak Your Name
And I am in Glory
Glory shines upon me.

Index

Afterword

There's an ecstatic experience that can happen when a person worships. I'm sure there's a scientific reason that has to do with serotonin or something, but there is an amazing effect that can happen when one worships or praises that changes a life. At that time, you have a definite 'suspension of disbelief'. The outpouring of your emotions becomes cathartic. For all intents and purposes, you become an empty vessel. You reach out to the wondrous, and the wondrous reaches back and fills you. It floods your being with the most incredible, indescribable feeling. When the experience is over, you end up exhausted, drained, and energized at the same time.

I don't think there has to be a religious practice involved to experience an ecstatic moment. Any spiritual experience can lead us there. Religion is the path we're most familiar with. It can easily lead us to worship, praise, and thanksgiving. I think it comes down to a spiritual experience, whether through happiness, or praise, or even listening to music which uplifts us, creating this experience which makes us one with the All.

I was raised holy-roller fundamentalist; indoctrinated from infancy. It was a great foundation for my life. I was a 'true believer' and I loved my church, the music, the prayers, and the feelings I got when I prayed. Over time, my spiritual path changed, my prayers changed, and how I view God changed. Now I pray to Life, or I Am, because I can't fathom a molecule in this world without God, in whatever form It takes, being in its entirety.

What I focus on now is worship, which is another word for adoration, and thankfulness, especially thankfulness. Most of my prayers are about praise, and usually sound something like this: thank you, thank you, thank you, thank you, thank you, thank you, thank you, thank you, thank you, thank you, thank you, thank you, thank you, thank you, thank you, thank you, thank you, thank you. It's heartfelt, and how can I not feel joy after that? Of course, I also tend to say thank you when I see a magnificent tree, or when someone doesn't run me down with their car, or when I'm simply happy. And, I've found that when life hurts too much to say anything, being thankful makes a difference.

The part of all this I haven't mentioned is blessing. Because sometimes life does just hurt too much, and sometimes I can't seem to get there from here. So in between those times I fill my life with as much blessing as I can get. The word blessing can mean anything from feeling fortunate, to happy, to being endowed with divine favor. So, you can pick your flavor: religious or not.

The best thing about blessings is that they are everywhere. I am blessed in so many ways, by so many things: unexpected kindnesses, my abilities, my lack of aptitude for things I don't like to do, finding a discarded bird's egg, having so many years with my darling, and pretty much anything else I decide to feel blessed by. I don't stop there—I bless everyone and everything with my personal blessings. My non-Christian friends think I'm being Christian; my Christian friends think I'm doing it wrong; I smile and bless them anyway.

Made in the USA
Middletown, DE
21 March 2019